To:

_____

From:

_____

Date:

_____

Your *Finances,*
God's Promises

A Dozen Biblically-based Principles for Achieving Financial Security

YOUR
FINANCES,

GOD'S
PROMISES

*A Dozen Biblically-based Principles for
Achieving Financial Security*

FAMILY
CHRISTIAN
PRESS

ISBN 1404184317

Printed in the United States of America
Cover Design: Nick Long
Page Layout: Bart Dawson

1 2 3 4 5 6 7 8 9 10 • 03 04 05 06 07 08 09 10

*For Everyone
Who Puts God First*

TABLE OF CONTENTS

INTRODUCTION

God has the final word on everything, including your finances. The Bible contains principles for financial security which, if followed, will lead to long-term financial independence for you and your family. But in order to follow the Bible's instructions, you must take the time to understand the Biblical laws that apply to your own economic well-being. This little book is intended to help.

You live in a highly complicated world that is definitely *not* designed to help you achieve financial independence. To the contrary, most of the messages you hear and see each day are intended to induce you to *spend* money, not to *save* it. But, in order to *have* money, you must not only learn how to earn it, you must also learn how to *keep* it. And, as we all know, keeping money is often harder than earning it.

This book contains ideas that can revolutionize the way that you think about money *and* the way that you handle your personal finances. If you take these ideas to heart and apply them to your life, you will live wisely and well, and that's good.

But matters of this earth, including your financial well-being, are of no importance when compared with matters of spiritual well-being. So place God at the center of your heart, and trust Christ for your personal salvation. Then, obey God's Word in every aspect of your life, including your finances. When you do, God will bless you, and you, in turn, will bless others.

Money is a tool, nothing more. It is a tool that can and should be used by you to improve your own life and the lives of your loved ones. If you approach the use of money in a disciplined, thoughtful way, *and* if you live by God's commandments, you will be surprised at the gifts that He has in store for you. So trust God, obey His commandments . . . and then start unwrapping all those gifts!

A Note to Readers

A wise man will hear and increase in learning, and a man of understanding will acquire wise counsel.

—

Proverbs 1:5 NASB

The financial advice in this book is general in nature, and your circumstances are specific to you. For that reason, we strongly suggest that you consult a competent financial professional *before* making dramatic changes in your own financial circumstances. Do not depend upon this book—or any other book, for that matter—to be the sole source of your investment advice. Instead, consider Proverbs 1:5 and seek wise counsel from a variety of sources before making a major decision, financial or otherwise.

Principle #1

Live According to God's Wisdom

Blessed is the man who finds wisdom,
the man who gains understanding . . . .

—

PROVERBS 3:13 NIV

As Christians, we are tempted to divide our lives into two categories: "spiritual" and "secular." We are tempted to spend Sunday mornings and Wednesday nights devoting ourselves to our spiritual needs while spending the rest of the week focused on material concerns. But to do so is wrong. God instructs us to obey His commandments at all times. And, we demonstrate our love for our Creator by obeying His laws (*1 John 5:3 KJV*).

The Bible has much to say about personal conduct, including financial matters. As believers, we should read God's Word *and* we should live by it. When we do, we become more moderate, more temperate, more thoughtful, more generous, and more disciplined.

Achieving financial security is a matter of applying God's wisdom to everyday life. Wisdom is the foundation upon which financial independence is built. But wisdom, especially as it relates to financial matters, doesn't come easily for most of us. Why? Because, as imperfect human beings living in a temptation-filled world, we see so many things that we want, and we want those things *now*.

God's Word teaches the twin virtues of moderation and patience. When we spend money moderately—and when we wait patiently until we can afford the things that we buy—we free ourselves from the chains of debt and worry. And that's exactly what God's Holy Word instructs us to do.

Do you seek financial security for yourself and for your family? Then make yourself a student of God's Word. Study it carefully and apply it to every aspect of your life, including your finances. You'll soon discover that God's way beats the world's way every day of the week . . . not just on Sundays.

GOD'S WORD ON WISDOM

But if any of you lacks wisdom,
let him ask of God, who gives to all
generously and without reproach, and
it will be given to him.

JAMES 1:5 NASB

Wise men store up knowledge, but
the mouth of a fool invites ruin.

PROVERBS 10:14 NIV

He who walks with the wise
grows wise.

PROVERBS 13:20 NIV

THOSE WHO ARE WISE WILL SHINE
LIKE THE BRIGHTNESS OF
THE HEAVENS.

—

DANIEL 12:3 NIV

GOD'S WORD ON
THE NEED FOR PATIENCE

Patience is better than strength.

PROVERBS 16:32 ICB

Wait on the LORD, and
he shall save thee.

PROVERBS 20:22 KJV

Yet the LORD longs to be gracious to
you; he rises to show you compassion.
For the LORD is a God of justice.
Blessed are all who wait for him!

ISAIAH 30:18 NIV

A MAN'S WISDOM
GIVES HIM PATIENCE.

—

PROVERBS 19:11 NIV

GOD'S WORD ON THE NEED FOR MODERATION AND SELF-CONTROL

Be above reproach . . . temperate, prudent, respectable, hospitable, able to teach, not addicted to wine or pugnacious, but gentle, peaceable, free from the love of money.

1 TIMOTHY 3:2-3 NASB

Add to your faith virtue; and to virtue, knowledge; and to knowledge, temperance; and to temperance, patience; and to patience, godliness; and to godliness, brotherly kindness; and to brotherly kindness, charity.

2 PETER 1:5-7 KJV

Do you not know that those who run in a race all run, but only one receives the prize? Run in such a way that you may win. Everyone who competes in the games exercises self-control in all things.

1 CORINTHIANS 9:24-25 NASB

HUMBLE YOURSELVES THEREFORE
UNDER THE MIGHTY HAND OF GOD,
THAT HE MAY EXALT YOU
IN DUE TIME.
—
1 PETER 5:6 KJV

Will regular readings of your Bible make you a financial genius? Probably not. The Bible is God's Holy Word; it is intended not as a tool for prosperity, but as a tool for salvation. Nevertheless, the Bible *can* teach you how to become a more disciplined, patient person. And as you become a more disciplined person in other aspects of your life, you will also become more disciplined in the management of your personal finances.

So study God's Word and use it as your guidebook for living, and while you're at it, consider the following:

FINANCIAL TIP #1: **Read, Read, Read**: The best way to learn about any subject is to read a variety of books. If this little book is your first exposure to the world of personal financial management, make sure that it's not your last.

—

FINANCIAL TIP #2: **Do the Math**: If you don't already have one, it's time to sit down and write down your personal budget. You'll read more about this in the next chapter.

—

FINANCIAL TIP #3: **When in Doubt, Don't**: Money is hard to earn and incredibly easy to spend. If you're not absolutely certain that you have the financial wherewithal to buy something, don't buy it!

—

FINANCIAL TIP #4: **Stuff 101**: The world says, "Buy more stuff." God says, "Stuff isn't important." Believe God.

FINANCIAL TIP #5: Discipline Is Not a Four-letter Word: Exercising financial discipline should never be viewed as an imposition or as a form of punishment; far from it. Discipline is the means by which you can take control of your life (which, by the way, is far better than letting your life control *you*).

—

FINANCIAL TIP # 6: Simplicity Is Beautiful: If your mailbox is overflowing with credit card bills and your bank balance is approaching single digits, it's officially time to simplify your life. But before you unload that seldom-used food processor at your next yard sale, toss your credit cards into the blender and push "Liquefy."

—

FINANCIAL TIP #7: Patience Is Genius: Are there things in this life that you'd like to own? Be patient. If you work hard, if you save your money diligently, and if you trust God's will, you'll have many of the things you want and *all* of the things you really need.

ADD TO YOUR FAITH VIRTUE;
AND TO VIRTUE, KNOWLEDGE.

—

2 PETER 1:5 KJV

AND IN CONCLUSION: GOD'S WORD

By wisdom a house is built, and
through understanding it is established;
through knowledge its rooms are filled
with rare and beautiful treasures.

—

PROVERBS 24:3-4 NIV

PRINCIPLE #2

SPEND LESS
THAN YOU MAKE

———◆———

The plans of the diligent lead to profit
as surely as haste leads to poverty.

—

PROVERBS 21:5 NIV

You've probably heard this advice on thousands of occasions: "Spend less than you make." It sounds so easy, but it can be so hard. After all, we live in a world that is filled to the brim with wonderful things to buy and wonderful people telling us that we need to buy those things. But sometimes, our desires for more and better stuff can overload our ability to pay for the things we want. That's when troubles arise.

The answer to the problem of overspending is straightforward. First, we must earn money through honest work for which we are well suited; then, we must spend less than we earn (and save the rest intelligently). The best way to track income and expenses is with a written budget.

FINANCIAL TIP #8: **Budgeting Basics 101**: Your budget should be: realistic, clearly written down on paper, created in cooperation with your spouse (if you have one), and reviewed regularly.

—

FINANCIAL TIP #9: **If You're Not Saving Money, Your Budget Isn't Working**: All too often, our written budgets contain too much hope and too little reality: It's easy to deceive ourselves with budgets that don't reflect the reality of our particular situations. If you have a budget that reflects positive cash flow but a bank account that contains little or no cash, it's time for a reality check.

FINANCIAL TIP #10: **Establish a Cash Cushion**: How much cash do you need in your "rainy day" fund? That depends upon your current income, your current level of expenses, and the time that it might take you to find new work if you were to find yourself "between" jobs. Sit down with your spouse (if you have one) and determine how much cash you need in your account to sleep comfortably at night. And then don't buy another big ticket item until you've saved that amount.

—

FINANCIAL TIP #11: **If Your Income Is Variable, Budget and Spend Conservatively**: If your income depends heavily upon sales commissions, bonuses, overtime, or profit sharing, don't assume that next year will be as good as last year. The more your income changes, the more conservative should be your spending habits. And never spend variable income until the check has cleared.

FINANCIAL TIP #12: **Let the Computer Crunch the Numbers, Write the Checks, and Balance the Checkbook**: If you own a home computer, and if you write more than a few checks each month, it may be time to invest in personal accounting software. If used properly, this powerful financial tool can be incredibly helpful. And besides, a good accounting package now costs less than a hundred bucks. Don't we live in an amazing world?

—

FINANCIAL TIP #13: **Leave Room in Your Budget for Surprises**: Unless you have clairvoyant powers (and you don't), it is wise to leave room in your budget for unexpected little surprises.

Thoughts on Budgeting

About the time we can make
the ends meet,
somebody moves the ends.

HERBERT HOOVER

Budgeting is telling your money where
to go instead of asking it
where it went.

JOHN MAXWELL

Plan your work and your life.
Without a system,
you'll feel swamped.

NORMAN VINCENT PEALE

THE BEST PLAN IS ONLY A PLAN,
THAT IS, GOOD INTENTIONS, UNLESS
IT DEGENERATES INTO WORK.

—

PETER DRUCKER

Thoughts on
Income and Expenditures

Do not count your chickens
before they hatch.

AESOP

Draw your salary before spending it.

GEORGE ADE

Never spend your money
before you have it.

THOMAS JEFFERSON

MONEY IS A TERRIBLE MASTER BUT
AN EXCELLENT SERVANT.

—

P. T. BARNUM

AND IN CONCLUSION:
GOD'S WORD

A faithful man shall abound
with blessings: but he that maketh haste
to be rich shall not be innocent.
—

PROVERBS 28:20 KJV

Principle #3

Anticipate Risks

—◆—

The prudent see danger and take refuge, but the simple keep going and suffer from it.

—

Proverbs 27:12 NIV

The world in which we live is full of uncertainties. Although we cannot control the future, we can and should plan for it; to do otherwise is to invite havoc into our own lives, not to mention the lives of our family members.

Thankfully, we live in a world where the financial effects of risk can be managed through the use of insurance. Here are some things to consider.

FINANCIAL TIP #14: Insurance 101: You need insurance. Period. At a minimum, here's what you need:

1. Enough life insurance to provide for your family in the event of your death;
2. Sufficient health insurance to provide for you and for those under your care;
3. An inexpensive disability policy to augment Social Security benefits;
4. Auto insurance (if you own a car);
5. Home insurance (if you own a home) *or* renter's insurance (to cover your personal possessions).

And, of course, don't hesitate to ask an expert to look at all your insurance needs in detail.

FINANCIAL TIP #15: Insurance 201: **Shop Around**: Over your lifetime, you'll spend a surprisingly large percentage of your income on insurance. Insurance prices are highly variable. To make sure that you're not overpaying, shop around *before* you buy *and* when you renew policies.

—

FINANCIAL TIP #16: **The Great Life Insurance Dilemma—Term Versus Whole Life:** Term life insurance is the kind of insurance that provides death benefits only. A "whole life" insurance policy (and other similar types of policies) is, in essence, a term policy with certain additional investment features added on for good measure. For obvious reasons, whole life policies usually cost substantially more than term policies. In most cases, you'll be better off purchasing term insurance (especially if you need lots of insurance at a cheap price). But, whole life policies do have certain advantages, especially if you wish to lock in a particular premium payment for the rest of your life. When in doubt about which type of policy is best for you, check with a professional advisor whom you trust.

FINANCIAL TIP #17: **Deductibles, Deductibles, Deductibles**: The term "deductible" refers to the amount of money that you will pay out of your own pocket when an insured event occurs. All other things being equal, the higher your deductible, the lower should be your insurance premium. If your premiums are going through the roof, ask your insurance broker to investigate the possibility of raising your deductibles. But remember: if your deductible payments are higher, your "rainy day fund" should be higher, too.

—

FINANCIAL TIP #18: **Diversify, Diversify, Diversify**: In today's fast-changing, topsy-turvy world, *don't even think about* putting all your eggs in a single basket. There's more in this book about *that* topic later.

A DANGER FORESEEN
IS HALF AVOIDED.

—

THOMAS FULLER

AND IN CONCLUSION: GOD'S WORD

A prudent person foresees
the danger ahead and takes precautions;
the simpleton goes blindly on and
suffers the consequences.

—

PROVERBS 22:3 NLT

PRINCIPLE #4

UNDERSTAND DEBT

———◆———

The borrower is servant to the lender.

—

PROVERBS 22:7 NIV

We live in a world that has become so reliant upon debt that our entire economy depends upon it. How many automobiles would dealers sell if there were no car loans? Not many. And how many businesses would cease operations if, tomorrow morning, their short term credit lines were called in by the banks? Plenty! Face it: we live in a world that is addicted to debt, but you needn't be. Just because our world revolves around borrowed money doesn't mean that you must do likewise.

If you're already living beyond your means and borrowing to pay for the privilege, then you know that sleepless nights and stress-filled days are the psychological payments that must be extracted from those who buy too much "now" in hopes that they can pay for those things "later." Unfortunately, "later" always arrives *sooner* rather than later, and that's when the trouble begins.

What's the solution? For starters, consider the following advice:

FINANCIAL TIP #19: **When You Finance Your Purchase, You Pay More**: All other things being equal, you will usually pay more when you purchase items on credit. If you want the best price for an item, whether it's a new car, a new suit, or a new house, bring cash *and* be willing to negotiate with the seller. If you want to pay more, bring no cash and be willing to accept the seller's "easy" terms (but don't forget that easy credit is an oxymoron).

—

FINANCIAL TIP #20: **All Too Often, the True Interest Rate Is Hidden in the Small Print**: Here in the real world, it's sad but true: the smaller the print, the higher the cost. Beware of obligations that require you to commit yourself to a long string of payments. This includes "rent to own" plans.

FINANCIAL TIP #21: **Never Borrow Money for Things That You Expect to Go Down in Value**: Okay, almost never. If you absolutely need to borrow money to buy basic transportation in order to drive to and from work, that's acceptable ("basic transportation" means a serviceable, affordable used car, not a brand new one).

—

FINANCIAL TIP #22: **The Partial List of Things You Should Not Borrow Money to Purchase**: Don't borrow money to buy gifts, trips, boats, motorcycles, meals at restaurants, jewelry, artwork, or clothes, for starters.

FINANCIAL TIP #23: **Credit Cards 101: Don't Use Credit Cards to Finance Your Lifestyle**: Credit cards should never be confused with banks. If you want a business loan for a legitimate purpose, go to a lending institution. If you need a mortgage on your home, call a reputable broker. But if you're about to buy a consumable item using a credit card, be sure that you can pay for it when the bill comes due.

—

FINANCIAL TIP #24: **Credit Cards 201: How to Tell If You're Not Using Your Credit Cards Wisely**: If your credit card balance is more than you can comfortably pay each time the bill comes due, then you're charging too much.

FINANCIAL TIP #25: **What to Do If You Can't Seem to Manage Your Credit Card Debt**: If you can't manage your credit cards responsibly, cut them up today and pay off your account balances as quickly as you can. Then, vow never to own another credit card as long as you live (a debit card should become your "card of choice").

BUT THERE'S MORE . . .

Okay, all debt is bad, right? Wrong! Upon further review, it's okay to borrow money for things that have a high likelihood of going up in value *if* you completely understand that investment *and* you exercise a reasonable amount of control over it. The best investment that fits that description is the home you live in.

FINANCIAL TIP #26: **A Mortgage on Your Home Is Okay . . . Within Reason:** Unless you were born with a substantial trust fund—and if you were, you're probably not reading this book—you will need to borrow money to purchase your home. And because home ownership has many benefits, you're probably wise to do so *if* you use common sense. Don't try to "max out" your mortgage by borrowing every penny that you can. And don't load yourself down with a second mortgage that can further crimp your financial style. Instead, wait until you have saved enough money to make a substantial down payment, and don't buy a more expensive home than you can afford.

WARNINGS ABOUT DEBT

Debt is like any other trap.
It is easy enough to get into but
hard enough to get out of.

JOSH BILLINGS

Too many people buy things on
the "lay-awake" plan.

DAVE RAMSEY

Debt shortens life.

JOSEPH JOUBERT

HOME LIFE CEASES TO BE FREE
AND BEAUTIFUL AS SOON AS
IT IS FOUNDED ON BORROWING
AND DEBT.

—

HENRIK IBSEN

THOUGHTS ON BEING DEBT-FREE

It is better to go to bed supperless
than rise in debt.

BEN FRANKLIN

I care not so much what I am to others
as what I am to myself. I will be rich
by myself, and not by borrowing.

MICHEL DE MONTAIGNE

Few things in life exceed
the satisfaction of being debt free.

WILLIAM CRISWELL

WHAT CAN BE ADDED TO
THE HAPPINESS OF A MAN WHO IS
IN HEALTH, WHO IS OUT OF DEBT,
AND WHO HAS A CLEAR
CONSCIENCE?

—

ADAM SMITH

OTHER PEOPLE'S DEBT

Do not cosign another person's note
or put up a guarantee for someone else's
loan. If you can't pay it, even your bed
will be snatched from under you.

PROVERBS 22:7 NLT

If you're considering obligating
yourself to someone else's obligation, it's
time to reconsider. And while you're
reconsidering, consider the following

FINANCIAL TIP #27: Cosigning 101: If
you're thinking about cosigning someone
else's note, remember that once you sign
your name to the dotted line, your liability is very real indeed. So, if you are about
to cosign someone else's obligation, follow this simple advice: don't do it.

FINANCIAL TIP #28: **Cosigning 201**: If you have already cosigned on someone else's note, it may be too late to change anything . . . this time! Still, it is never too late to consider this passage from God's Word:

> My child, if you co-sign a loan for a friend or guarantee the debt of someone you hardly know, if you have trapped yourself by your agreement and are caught by what you said, quick, get out of it if you possibly can! You have placed yourself at your friend's mercy. Now swallow your pride; go and beg to have your name erased. Don't put it off. Do it now! Don't rest until you do. Save yourself like a deer escaping from a hunter, like a bird fleeing from a net.
>
> PROVERBS 6:1-5 NLT

AND IN CONCLUSION:
GOD'S WORD

Pay all your debts, except the debt
of love for others. You can never finish
paying that! If you love your neighbor,
you will fulfill all the requirements
of God's law.

—

ROMANS 13:8 NLT

PRINCIPLE #5

FIND THE RIGHT JOB

⟨⬦⟩

Whatever you do, work at it
with all your heart, as working for
the Lord, not for men.
—

COLOSSIANS 3:23 NIV

In the good old days, you might go to work for a company, work there for thirty years, and retire with both a gold watch *and* a decent pension. But these aren't the good old days; these are the good *new* days, and the rules have changed.

Today, even if you're working for an established company, you cannot be certain that you'll be working there when you retire, even if you're the best employee in the history of capitalism! Why? In today's rapid-fire business environment, even the very best employees may be swept out on the tides of change. That's why today's perfect job may be tomorrow's fond memory. And that's why you'd best prepare yourself for the inevitable changes that are probably right around the corner. Here are a few ideas.

FINANCIAL TIP #29: **Keep Looking for Work That You Love Until You Find It**: In the long run, you'll be more successful if you discover a career that, for you, is a blessing not a burden.

—

FINANCIAL TIP #30: **Make Sure That Your Personality Fits the Work You Have Chosen**: Even if the job pays well, it's not a good job if it's not a good fit. How can you tell? If you're having trouble showing up at work, if you're having trouble completing your core assignments, or if you can't get along with your coworkers, then it's probably time to look elsewhere.

—

FINANCIAL TIP #31: **Never Stop Learning**: The technology snowball has turned into an avalanche. Your job will not be unaffected, so keep training yourself. And don't wait for your employer to decide that it's time for you to receive training. Start learning on your own time, and keep learning every day that you live.

FINANCIAL TIP #32: A Second Job? When in Doubt, Check It Out: What if your regular job doesn't pay enough to meet your financial needs? If so, perhaps it's time to find a second one. After all, nowhere in the Bible does it mention the 40-hour workweek. So, if you're hard at work on job #1, don't forget that job #2 is also a possibility, especially if you're paying off debts.

—

FINANCIAL TIP #33: If You Want to Make a Great Investment, Invest in Yourself: As Ben Franklin observed, "An investment in knowledge always pays the best interest."

Ideas about Lifetime Learning

To make headway, improve your head.

B. C. Forbes

I learned the importance of self-education. Once you realize that the learning is up to you, you have the right attitude to succeed in school and beyond.

Tony Bennett

Never stop acquiring specialized knowledge.

Napoleon Hill

The illiterate of the future will not be those who cannot read and write, but those who cannot learn, unlearn, and relearn.

Alvin Toffler

IN A TIME OF DRASTIC CHANGE,
IT IS THE LEARNERS WHO INHERIT
THE FUTURE.

—

ERIC HOFFER

IDEAS ABOUT WORK

The most unhappy of all men is the
man who cannot tell what he is going
to do, has got no work cut out for him
in the world, and does not go into it.
For work is the grand cure of all the
maladies and miseries that ever beset
mankind—honest work, which you
intend getting done.

THOMAS CARLYLE

Never let your work drive you.
Master it and keep it in
complete control.

BOOKER T. WASHINGTON

The person who excels is the person
who does something for the pure love
of it and doesn't think of the commercial
consequences. If you do something,
do it right, and the finances will usually
take care of themselves.

CHET ATKINS

69

IDEAS ABOUT FINDING WORK THAT YOU ENJOY

Success is being truly happy
at what you do.

TOMMY LASORDA

As one gets on in years, there is
a satisfaction in doing a thing for
the sake of doing it.

RUSSELL CONWELL

If you want to be successful,
it's just this simple:
Know what you're doing.
Love what you're doing.
And believe in what you're doing.

WILL ROGERS

GET ABSOLUTELY ENTHRALLED
WITH SOMETHING. THROW
YOURSELF INTO IT WITH ABANDON.
GET OUT OF YOURSELF.
BE SOMEBODY. DO SOMETHING.

—

NORMAN VINCENT PEALE

God's Words about Work

Work hard so God can approve you.
Be a good worker, one who does not
need to be ashamed and who correctly
explains the word of truth.

2 Timothy 2:15 NLT

But as for you, be strong and do not
give up, for your work will be rewarded.

2 Chronicles 15:7 NIV

Take a lesson from the ants,
you lazybones. Learn from their ways
and be wise! Even though they have no
prince, governor, or ruler to make them
work, they labor hard all summer,
gathering food for the winter. But you,
lazybones, how long will you sleep?
When will you wake up?

Proverbs 6:6-9 NLT

WHATEVER YOUR HAND FINDS
TO DO, DO IT
WITH ALL YOUR MIGHT . . . .
—
ECCLESIASTES 9:10 NIV

EVEN WHILE WE WERE WITH YOU,
WE GAVE YOU THIS RULE:
"WHOEVER DOES NOT WORK
SHOULD NOT EAT."

—

2 THESSALONIANS 3:10 NLT

Don't work hard only when your
master is watching and then shirk
when he isn't looking; work hard and
with gladness all the time, as though
working for Christ, doing the will
of God with all your hearts.

EPHESIANS 6:6-7 TLB

Be strong and courageous, and
do the work. Do not be afraid or
discouraged, for the LORD God,
my God, is with you.

1 CHRONICLES 28:20 NIV

He did it with all his heart,
and prospered.

2 CHRONICLES 31:21 KJV

AND IN CONCLUSION: GOD'S WORD

Each will receive his own reward
according to his own labor.
Each man's work will become evident.
—

1 CORINTHIANS 3:8,13 NASB

PRINCIPLE #6

SPEND WISELY

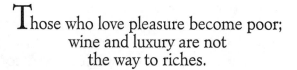

Those who love pleasure become poor;
wine and luxury are not
the way to riches.

—

PROVERBS 21:17 NLT

LESS IS MORE:

Spending money is an incredibly easy thing to do. After all, the shopping malls and discount stores are filled to the ceilings with attractively packaged items, all of which were created for a single purpose: so that we, the consuming public, might buy them.

But when we spend more than we should—when we become overly absorbed with the acquisition of things— complications arise. Each new acquisition costs money or time, often both. To further complicate matters, many items can be purchased, not with real money, but with something much more insidious: debt. Debt—especially consumer debt used to purchase items that immediately go down in value—is a modern-day form of indentured servitude.

If you're looking for a sure-fire, time-tested way to simplify your life and thereby improve your world, learn to control your possessions before they control you. Purchase only those things that make a significant contribution to your well-being and the well-being of your family. Never spend more than you make. Understand the folly in buying consumer goods on credit. Never use credit cards as a way of financing your lifestyle.

Ask yourself this simple question: "Do I own my possessions, or do they own me?" If you don't like the answer you receive, make an ironclad promise to stop acquiring and start divesting. As you simplify your life, you'll be amazed at the things you can do without. You'll be pleasantly surprised at the sense of satisfaction that accompanies your newfound moderation. And you'll understand first-hand that when it comes to material possessions, less truly is more.

SPENDING WISELY

For most of us, the key to financial security is the ability to control expenses. But, there's a catch: we can't stop spending entirely because we need to make purchases in order to provide for the basic necessities of daily life. The challenge, of course, is to make our hard-earned dollars go farther. Here are some tips:

FINANCIAL TIP #34: **Plan Ahead:** If you wait till the last minute, you invariably pay more. But, if you plan ahead, you can shop at the most affordable stores and you can buy things on sale.

—

FINANCIAL TIP #35: **Coupons?** Clipping coupons is a great way to save money if you only clip coupons for the items that you really need.

FINANCIAL TIP #36: **Quantity Saves:** If you're buying paper towels one roll at a time, you're probably paying too much. So, if you have the space in your home, buy non-perishable goods in quantity.

—

FINANCIAL TIP #37: **Off-season Purchases Save Money:** The best time to buy a bathing suit is in September, and the best time to buy a winter coat is in February.

—

FINANCIAL TIP #38: **More Convenience Usually Costs More:** When you drop in and buy a bag of chips at the local convenience store, you'll often pay twice as much as you would at the local grocery store. Think about it.

FINANCIAL TIP # 39: **Shop Around:** If you're about to make a major purchase, you'll be amazed at the variability of prices. Shop around, and don't forget to check the Internet.

—

FINANCIAL TIP #40: **Negotiate, Negotiate, Negotiate:** If you're interested in purchasing something, make an offer. The worst thing the seller can say is no, and who knows? He or she might say yes. P.S.: cash offers are much more attractive to sellers, and that's another good reason to save your cash for those times when you really need it.

—

FINANCIAL TIP # 41: **Generic?** Absolutely! Today, almost every retail product has its generic equivalent. Often, these generic products are almost identical to higher-priced brand-name products. Do yourself a favor and check out the generic equivalents of the products you buy.

FINANCIAL TIP #42: Wholesale Clubs? Yes, but . . . Wholesale clubs are wonderful if you use them often enough to justify their annual fees. And if you decide to join a wholesale club, check out all its services, including insurance, long distance phone cards, and automotive products, to name but a few.

—

FINANCIAL TIP # 43: Today's Amazing Cost-Cutting World: In addition to wholesale clubs, there are a wide range of low-cost alternatives to traditional retailers. If you snoop around, you'll probably find stores in your community that sell all sorts of things at reduced prices. Check them out.

FINANCIAL TIP # 44: **Understand the Bills You Pay:** We live in a world where every company, or so it seems, is "fee happy." And all those little fees can add up. When you receive a bill, especially one from a big company, watch for "transaction fees," "access fees," "roaming charges," "user fees," "prep fees," or any charge that ends with the word "passthrough." If you can't have the fee waived, you may want to consider changing to another vendor.

WEALTH IS SOMETHING ENTRUSTED
TO US BY GOD, SOMETHING GOD
DOESN'T WANT US TO TRUST.
HE WANTS US TO TRUST HIM.

—

WARREN WIERSBE

THE IMPORTANCE OF CONTROLLING YOUR EXPENSES

Economy is half the battle of life; it is not so hard to earn money as it is to spend it well.

C. H. SPURGEON

The best money advice I ever got was from my father. He said, "Don't spend anything unless you have to."

DINAH SHORE

Beware of little expenses. A small leak will sink a big ship.

BEN FRANKLIN

A FIXED INCOME IS WHAT'S LEFT
OVER AFTER YOU'VE FIXED
THE WASHING MACHINE, THE TV,
THE CAR, AND THE KID'S BIKE.
—
DAVE RAMSEY

AND IN CONCLUSION:
GOD'S WORD

The diligent make use
of everything they find.

—

PROVERBS 12:27 NLT

PRINCIPLE #7

ESTABLISH RESERVES

———◆◇◆———

The wise have wealth and luxury, but
fools spend whatever they get.

—

PROVERBS 21:20 NLT

Once you have established a rainy day fund, should you plow all the rest of your money into mutual funds and consumable goods? Of course not. Your personal savings account should continue to grow even after you've socked away enough cash to tide you over for a few months.

How much should you save? In some countries, where costs are substantially higher than they are in America, the savings rate exceeds 15%. You should save at least 10% of your take-home pay, for starters. And if you're in a high-income bracket, you should save even more.

THE HABIT OF SAVING IS ITSELF
AN EDUCATION; IT FOSTERS EVERY
VIRTUE, TEACHES SELF-DISCIPLINE,
CULTIVATES THE SENSE OF ORDER,
AND BROADENS THE MIND.
—
T. T. MUNGER

ANY FOOL CAN WASTE,
ANY FOOL CAN MUDDLE,
BUT IT TAKES SOMETHING OF
A MAN TO SAVE, AND THE MORE
HE SAVES, THE MORE OF
A MAN IT MAKES HIM.

—

RUDYARD KIPLING

PUT MONEY IN THY PURSE.

—

WILLIAM SHAKESPEARE

AND IN CONCLUSION: GOD'S WORD

She carefully watches all that goes on in her household and does not have to bear the consequences of laziness.

—

PROVERBS 31:27 NLT

PRINCIPLE #8

INVEST WISELY

———◆———

The man who had received the five
talents brought the other five. "Master,"
he said, "you entrusted me with five
talents. See, I have gained five more."
His master replied, "Well done, good and
faithful servant! You have been faithful
with a few things; I will put you in charge
of many things. Come and share your
master's happiness."

—

MATTHEW 25:20-21 NIV

Once you've paid off all your debts (except, perhaps, for your home mortgage), and once you've built up a reasonable balance in your savings account, it's time to start planning seriously for the future. But how should you invest? Here are ten, time-tested tips for investing your hard-earned money:

10 Common Sense Commandments for Investing Your Money

Thou Shall Have an Investment Plan: If you don't know where you want to go, you'll probably never get there.

—

Thou Shall Diversify: Mutual funds are an excellent way to diversify your stock holdings, but you shouldn't invest all of your investment dollars in mutual funds; you should be diversified, even in your diversity.

—

Thou Shall Understand Thy Investments: You've got a good head on your shoulders; use it.

THOU SHALL PAY ATTENTION TO THY INVESTMENTS, BUT NOT TOO MUCH ATTENTION: Keep an eye on your passive investments, but don't waste hours upon hours in front of the TV watching the daily twists and turns of the stock market; for the average investor, excessive market watching is poor use of time and a distraction from more useful activities.

—

THOU SHALL INVEST CONSISTENTLY: Once you begin an investment program, stick with it through good markets and bad ones.

THOU SHALL NOT FOLLOW THE HERD, BUY INTO THE BUBBLE, OR ATTEMPT TO GET RICH QUICK: The herd mentality leads to economic bubbles. Economic bubbles lead to excessive greed. Excessive greed leads to spectacular losses (these losses are euphemistically called "market corrections" by the experts who probably sold all their stock when the prices were still outrageously high). Investors beware: those who attempt to get rich quick usually get poor instead. P.S. If it sounds too good to be true, it is.

—

THOU SHALL INVEST IN BUSINESSES THAT MAKE MONEY TODAY, NOT IN THOSE THAT HOPE TO MAKE MONEY SOME DAY: Whether you're investing in mutual funds or in interest-bearing instruments, make certain that your dollars are used to purchasing investments in proven companies (or governmental entities) that produce recurring cash flow.

THOU SHALL UNDERSTAND THE PRINCIPLE OF COMPOUND INTEREST: The term "compound interest" means reinvesting interest earnings so that the interest itself begins to earn interest. This phenomenon, also referred to as "compounding," has profound implications for your financial future *if* you're patient enough to let your savings grow. Study the power of compound interest and put that power to work for you.

—

THOU SHALL HAVE *EITHER* LIQUIDITY OR CONTROL: the term "liquidity" refers to speed with which an investment can be sold for cash. Certain investments, such as publicly traded stocks and bonds, have a high level of liquidity. Other investments (such as real estate, collectibles, or stock in small businesses) have markedly less liquidity. As a general rule, the less liquidity an investment has, the more control you should be able to exercise over it.

THOU SHALL INVEST IN THYSELF, TOO: Your most important financial investments are the time, energy, and money that you use to improve your own professional skills. Never stop investing in yourself *or* in the tools of your trade.

If You Own
Your Own Business

Owning your own business is a wonderful experience *if* you have, in no particular order: 1. A good business idea that works; 2. Enough time, energy, and capital to make the idea a reality; 3. accurate, timely accounting; 4. Enough discipline, perseverance, and courage to make it through the inevitable ups and downs of the business cycle. Whew!

But beware: even if you believe that your business can't fail (and rest assured that it can), you still owe it to yourself and to your family to diversify your investments beyond the ownership of your company. And what if your business doesn't earn enough money to allow you to save the cash needed to diversify your investments? Then perhaps you need to take a long, hard look at the operation of your business. After all, if your business can't pay you a reasonable wage for your efforts, then something about the business needs to be fixed.

GOD'S WORD ON BUSINESS ETHICS

The LORD abhors dishonest scales . . . .
PROVERBS 11:1 NIV

A fortune made by a lying tongue is
a fleeting vapor and a deadly snare.
PROVERBS 21:6 NIV

The wicked man earns deceptive wages,
but he who sows righteousness reaps
a sure reward.
PROVERBS 11:18 NIV

Thoughts on Investing

Money, says the proverb,
   makes money. When you have got
   a little, it is often easy to get more.

CHARLES DICKENS

Know what you own and
            why you own it.

PETER LYNCH

I never attempt to make money on
         the stock market. I buy on
   the assumption that they could close
         the market the next day and
         not reopen it for five years.

WARREN BUFFET

LARGE ENTERPRISES MAKE
THE FEW RICH, BUT THE MAJORITY
PROSPER ONLY THROUGH
THE CAREFULNESS AND
DETAIL OF THRIFT.

—

T. T. MUNGER

AND IN CONCLUSION:
GOD'S WORD

He who works his land will have abundant food, but the one who chases fantasies will have his fill of poverty.

—

PROVERBS 28:19 NIV

PRINCIPLE #9

SIMPLIFY YOUR LIFE

—◆—

Lay not up for yourselves treasures
upon earth, where moth and rust doth
corrupt, and where thieves break
through and steal: but lay up for
yourselves treasures in heaven, where
neither moth nor rust doth corrupt, and
where thieves do not break through
nor steal: for where your treasure is,
there will your heart be also.

—

MATTHEW 6:19-21 KJV

YOUR COMPLICATED WORLD

You live in a world where simplicity is in short supply. Think for a moment about the complexity of your everyday life and compare it to the lives of ancestors who lived only a hundred short years ago. Certainly, you are the beneficiary of many technological innovations, but those innovations have a price: in all likelihood, your world is highly complex. Consider the following:

1. From the moment you wake up in the morning until the time you lay your head on the pillow at night, you are the target of an endless stream of advertising information. Each message is intended to grab your attention in order to convince you to purchase things you didn't know you needed (and probably don't!).

2. Unless you happen to be a hermit living on a deserted island, you are a tax-paying citizen of a well-meaning but profoundly complicated government with excruciatingly complex tax and legal codes. A hundred years ago, income taxes, for all practical purposes, didn't exist; today, whether you realize it or not, you are a part-time bookkeeper for the government.

3. The pace of technology is ever quickening, perhaps leaving you with the uneasy feeling that the more you learn about high-tech matters, the more you need to learn.

4. You have, at your fingertips, a broad range of communication tools that can both improve you life and monopolize your time. Communication with your fellow human beings has never been cheaper or easier. With the advent of the Internet, you are a part of a global communication network with literally millions of potential callers vying for your attention.

5. Essential aspects of your life, including personal matters such as health care, are subject to an ever-increasing flood of rules and regulations from both the public and private sectors.

6. To complicate matters further, you are a member of this prosperous generation, and you probably have more money than your forefathers to spend on things that you may not really need. More spending means more items cluttering the landscape of your life.

Unless you take firm control of your time and your life, you may be overwhelmed by an ever-increasing tidal wave of complexity that threatens your happiness. The ideas that follow are intended to help you sort through the clutter, separate important matters from unimportant ones, and, in doing so, invest your time and effort on the things that are important to you, to your loved ones, and to your God.

FINANCIAL TIP #45: **Material Possessions 101**: On the grand stage of a well-lived life, material possessions should play a rather small role. Of course, we all need the basic necessities of life, but once we meet those needs for ourselves and for our families, the piling up of possessions can create more problems than it solves. Our real riches, of course, are not of this world. We are never really rich until we are rich in spirit.

—

FINANCIAL TIP #46: **Be Willing to Say No to Other People and to Yourself**: Lots of people want to sell you things, and perhaps you want very desperately to buy them. But until you learn the art of saying no to others and to yourself, you'll spend too much time, energy, and money on things that you may not be able to afford.

GOD'S WORD ON
THE RELATIVE IMPORTANCE OF
MATERIAL POSSESSIONS

A man's life does not consist in the abundance of his possessions.

LUKE 12:15 NIV

Therefore I say unto you, Take no thought for your life, what ye shall eat, or what ye shall drink; nor yet for your body, what ye shall put on. Is not the life more than meat, and the body than raiment? Behold the fowls of the air: for they sow not, neither do they reap, nor gather into barns; yet your heavenly Father feedeth them. Are ye not much better than they?

MATTHEW 6:25-26 KJV

JESUS ANSWERED, "IT IS WRITTEN: 'MAN DOES NOT LIVE BY BREAD ALONE, BUT ON EVERY WORD THAT COMES FROM THE MOUTH OF GOD.'"

—

MATTHEW 4:4 NIV

For we brought nothing into this world, and it is certain we can carry nothing out. And having food and raiment, let us be therewith content.

—

1 Timothy 6:7-8 KJV

UNCLUTTER YOUR MIND

A cluttered life is the physical mani-festation of a cluttered mind. Thus the first task in simplifying your life is to clarify your thoughts. In a cluttered world, it is difficult to distinguish imagined problems from real ones, big troubles from small ones, important tasks from trivial ones. If your thoughts become distorted, you'll soon find yourself caught up in an unproductive, unhappy maelstrom of wasted motion. The antidote to this frustration is simple: clear-headed, rational thinking.

Rational thought is elusive in the hustle and bustle of a fast-paced world. Clear thinking evades the person who is tired, stressed, or both. But without clear thinking, imprudent decisions are made and hastily acted upon, with predictably disappointing results.

A rested, quiet mind, on the other hand, is a powerful remedy to the everyday stresses that otherwise might interfere with sound decision-making. Thankfully, clear thinking is available to almost anyone who regularly takes a few minutes each morning to organize his or her thoughts. The early morning is the perfect time for prayer and for devotional readings. It is also the perfect time to inspire, educate, and organize oneself.

If you find yourself in extremely stressful circumstances, a regular time of contemplation and study may not be enough; you may wish to consult a trusted friend, a clergyman, or an impartial professional counselor. But for the everyday stresses of life, you'll find that a daily dose of early-morning meditation will allow you to thank your Creator, to organize your time, to clarify your objectives, and to motivate yourself to act upon your most important priorities. And if you find yourself worried about the concerns of the day, consider these familiar words from the sixth chapter of Matthew:

For this reason I say to you, do not be worried about your life, as to what you will eat or what you will drink; nor for your body, as to what you will put on. Is not life more than food, and the body more than clothing? Look at the birds of the air, that they do not sow, nor reap nor gather into barns, and yet your heavenly Father feeds them. Are you not worth much more than they? And who of you by being worried can add a single hour to his life? And why are you worried about clothing? Observe how the lilies of the field grow; they do not toil nor do they spin, yet I say to you that not even Solomon in all his glory clothed himself like one of these. But if God so clothes the grass of the field, which is alive today and tomorrow is thrown into the furnace, will He not much more clothe you? You of little faith! Do not worry then, saying, "What will we eat?" or "What will we drink?" or "What will we wear for clothing?" For the Gentiles eagerly seek all these things; for your heavenly Father knows that you need all these things. But seek first His kingdom and His righteousness, and all these things will be added to you. So do not worry about tomorrow; for tomorrow will care for itself. Each day has enough trouble of its own.

MATTHEW 6:25-34 NASB

Uncluttered Thinking

Never be afraid to sit awhile and think.

LORRAINE HANSBERRY

To solve a problem it is necessary
to think. It is necessary to think even
to decide what facts to collect.

ROBERT MAYNARD HUTCHINS

Good thoughts bear good fruit and
bad thoughts bear bad fruit.
And a man is his own gardener.

JAMES ALLEN

By a tranquil mind, I mean nothing
else than a mind well ordered.

MARCUS AURELIUS

AND IN CONCLUSION:
GOD'S WORD

Better a little with the fear of the LORD
than great wealth with turmoil.

—

PROVERBS 15:16 NIV

PRINCIPLE #10

SHARE
YOUR BLESSINGS

———◆———

Carry each other's burdens,
and in this way you will fulfill
the law of Christ.

—

GALATIANS 6:2 NIV

The thread of generosity is woven—completely and inextricably—into the very fabric of Christ's teachings. As He sent His disciples out to heal the sick and spread God's message of salvation, Jesus offered this guiding principle: "Freely you have received, freely give" (Matthew 10:8 NIV). The principle still applies. If we are to be disciples of Christ, we must give freely of our time, our possessions, and our love.

In 2 Corinthians 9, Paul reminds us that when we sow the seeds of generosity, we reap bountiful rewards in accordance with God's plan for our lives. Thus, we are instructed to give cheerfully and without reservation: "But this I say, He which soweth sparingly shall reap also sparingly; and he which soweth bountifully shall reap also bountifully. Every man according as he purposeth in his heart, so let him give; not grudgingly, or of necessity: for God loveth a cheerful giver" (vv. 6-7 KJV).

One of the greatest joys of financial independence is the ability to share your financial blessings with others. The more you earn *and* save, the more you'll have to share. So today, make this pledge and keep it: Be a cheerful, generous, courageous giver. The world needs your help, and you need the spiritual rewards that will be yours when you do.

GOD'S WORD ON KINDNESS

So, as those who have been chosen
of God, holy and beloved, put on a heart
of compassion, kindness, humility,
gentleness and patience.

COLOSSIANS 3:12 NASB

Be kind to one another, tender-hearted,
forgiving each other, just as God
in Christ also has forgiven you.

EPHESIANS 4:32 NASB

A kind man benefits himself, but
a cruel man brings trouble on himself.

PROVERBS 11:17 NIV

May God, who gives this patience and
encouragement, help you live in
complete harmony with each other—
each with the attitude of Christ Jesus
toward the other.

ROMANS 15:5 NLT

This is what the LORD Almighty says:
Judge fairly and honestly, and show
mercy and kindness to one another.

ZECHARIAH 7:9 NLT

Be peaceable, gentle, showing
every consideration for all men.

TITUS 3:2 NASB

GOD'S WORD ON GENEROSITY

The man with two tunics should share
with him who has none, and the one
who has food should do the same.

LUKE 3:11 NIV

And above all things have fervent
charity among yourselves: for charity
shall cover the multitude of sins.

1 PETER 4:8 KJV

I TELL YOU THE TRUTH,
WHATEVER YOU DID FOR ONE OF
THE LEAST OF THESE BROTHERS
OF MINE, YOU DID FOR ME.

—

MATTHEW 25:40 NIV

AND IN CONCLUSION:
GOD'S WORD ON TITHING

A tenth of the produce of the land,
whether grain or fruit, belongs
to the LORD and must be
set apart to him as holy.

—

LEVITICUS 27:30 NLT

PRINCIPLE #11

PLAN FOR DEATH

———◆———

I have fought the good fight, I have
finished the race, I have kept the faith.
—
2 TIMOTHY 4:7 NIV

If you've worked hard, worked smart, saved your money, and invested wisely, you won't die broke. Technically, the assets that you own are called your "estate." These assets represent what's left over from an entire life's work: yours! So why not decide where your assets will go? If you don't, the government will certainly decide for you, but that choice should be yours (not the courts'), and that's why you absolutely need a will.

If you die without a will, you will create confusion and hurt feelings among your family members. But a clear, unambiguous will can eliminate the confusion. So, you'll be doing your heirs a huge favor by spelling out your wishes.

If you've accepted Christ as your personal Savior, you're going to live forever in heaven. But you shouldn't neglect earthly duties, either. And so, consider the following tips *very* carefully.

FINANCIAL TIP #47: **Have a Written Will**: Most people die without a will. Don't be like most people.

—

FINANCIAL TIP #48: **If you don't have the money in your budget to hire a lawyer**: Suppose that you don't have a will but that you also don't have the money to hire a lawyer to help you draft one. Well, you can write out a will in your own handwriting, and when you sign it, it's official. So see, there's no excuse for not having a will, now, is there?

FINANCIAL TIP #49: Estate Planning 101: If you own a home or have other substantial assets that you want to pass on to the next generation, it's best to have a trusted professional help you draft your will so that you can make fully informed decisions about the ultimate distribution of your assets.

FINANCIAL TIP #50: Consider a Holographic Will: If you're planning on hiring a lawyer to draft your will, but you haven't done so yet, you should consider writing a holographic will. What's a holographic will? It's a will that is written in your own handwriting. And if you don't currently have a valid will, perhaps you should consider writing down your wishes *right now*. A holographic will is no substitute for a well-crafted instrument that has been drafted by a professional. But, a holographic is almost always better than nothing . . . lots better.

AND IN CONCLUSION:
GOD'S WORD

A good man leaves an inheritance
to his children's children.
—

PROVERBS 13:22 NASB

PRINCIPLE #12

TRUST GOD ALWAYS
AND
PLACE HIM FIRST

———◆———

Thou shalt have
no other gods before me.

—

EXODUS 20:3 KJV

The quest for financial security is a journey that leads us across many peaks and through a few unexpected valleys. When we reach the mountaintops, we find it easy to praise God and to give thanks. But, when we find ourselves in the dark valleys of life, when we face disappointment or financial hardship, it seems so much more difficult to trust God's perfect plan. But, trust Him we must.

As Christians, we can be comforted: Whether we find ourselves at the pinnacle of the mountain or the darkest depths of the valley, God is there. And we Christians have every reason to live courageously. After all, Christ has already won the ultimate battle on the cross at Calvary. Still, even dedicated Christians may find their courage tested by the inevitable disappointments that occur in the lives of believers and non-believers alike.

As you make the changes in your life that will result in financial security, remember this: The next time you find your courage tested to the limit (and it will be), lean upon God's promises. Trust His Son. Remember that God is always near and that He is your protector and your deliverer. Always.

No servant can serve
two masters. Either he will
hate the one and love
the other, or he will be devoted
to the one and despise
the other. You cannot
serve both God and Money.

—

Luke 16:13 NIV

TRUST IN YOUR MONEY
AND DOWN YOU GO!
BUT THE GODLY FLOURISH LIKE
LEAVES IN SPRING.

—

PROVERBS 11:28 NLT

THE STORY OF THE SERVANT WHO RECEIVED ONE TALENT

But the servant who received the one bag of gold dug a hole in the ground and hid the master's money for safekeeping. After a long time their master returned from his trip and called them to give an account of how they had used his money. The servant to whom he had entrusted the five bags of gold said, "Sir, you gave me five bags of gold to invest, and I have doubled the amount." The master was full of praise. "Well done, my good and faithful servant. You have been faithful in handling this small amount, so now I will give you many more responsibilities. Let's celebrate together!"

Next came the servant who had received the two bags of gold, with the report, "Sir, you gave me two bags of gold to invest, and I have doubled the amount." The master said, "Well done, my good and faithful servant. You have been faithful in handling this small amount, so now I will give you many more responsibilities. Let's celebrate together!"

Then the servant with the one bag of gold came and said, "Sir, I know you are a hard man, harvesting crops you didn't plant and gathering crops you didn't cultivate. I was afraid I would lose your money, so I hid it in the earth and here it is." But the master replied, "You wicked and lazy servant! You think I'm a hard man, do you, harvesting crops I didn't plant and gathering crops I didn't cultivate? Well, you should at least have put my money into the bank so I could have some interest. Take the money from this servant and give it to the one with the ten bags of gold. To those who use well what they are given, even more will be given, and they will have an abundance. But from those who are unfaithful, even what little they have will be taken away. Now throw this useless servant into outer darkness, where there will be weeping and gnashing of teeth."

MATTHEW 25:18-30 NLT

MOREOVER, WHEN GOD GIVES
ANY MAN WEALTH AND
POSSESSIONS, AND ENABLES HIM
TO ENJOY THEM, TO ACCEPT HIS LOT
AND BE HAPPY IN HIS WORK—
THIS IS A GIFT OF GOD.

—

ECCLESIASTES 5:19 NIV

AND IN CONCLUSION: GOD'S WORD

Your life should be free from
the love of money. Be satisfied with
what you have, for He Himself has said,
I will never leave you or forsake you.

—

HEBREWS 13:5 HCSB

AND A FEW FINAL THOUGHTS

It's Not a Financial Plan . . . It's a Way of Life

If you want to lose weight, don't go on a diet—change your lifestyle. And, if you want to create financial security for yourself and for your family, don't go on a financial diet; instead, adopt a new financial lifestyle.

For most Americans, it's normal to have a car note, a house note, a hefty amount of credit card debt, and a surprisingly skimpy bank balance. Don't be like them.

For most Americans, it's normal to spend now and to pay (or *hope to pay*) later. Don't be like them.

For most Americans, it's normal to buy the next new thing, and to pay for it with monthly payments that take a terrible toll both financially *and* emotionally. Don't be like them.

For most Americans, it's normal to spend lots of disposable income on things like cars, boats, travel, and clothes. And it's normal to sock far less money away in savings accounts. Don't be like them.

Instead, make a promise to yourself that you'll be the kind of responsible, disciplined spender that the Bible commands you to be. Make a promise to yourself that you'll save *first* and spend *later* (never vice-versa). And then, with the money you accumulate, give a generous portion to God's work here on earth while you build the kind of financial security that will give you peace of mind and a sense of satisfaction.

You live in the most prosperous society in the history of humanity. If you're sincerely ready to claim the financial rewards that can and should be yours, then today is the day that you must begin.

AND A FINAL FEW FINANCIAL TIPS:

ORGANIZE YOUR RECORDS: If you're a disorganized person, get over it. Disorganization leads to confusion, fuzzy thinking, missed opportunities, sloppy bookkeeping, and—when taken to its extreme—poverty.

—

THINK LONG TERM: If you wish to become a successful saver and an enlightened investor, you will need to exercise patience. If you think you want to be a speculator or a day trader, think again.

UP IN SMOKE: **The Cost of Addiction: Cigarettes, Alcohol, and Drugs**: If you smoke cigarettes, you're spending a small fortune in order to send yourself to an early grave. If you're a heavy drinker, you're spending a small fortune in order to filter out the beauty of God's creation. If you're foolish enough to take illegal drugs, you'll probably die broke, and soon. Addictions, of whatever kind, rob you of life, health, money, and peace of mind. If you're addicted to any of the aforementioned substances (or others that were not mentioned), speak with your pastor and seek out a 12-step program today . . . tomorrow may be too late.

THE HOUSE ALWAYS WINS: **The Financial Folly of Gambling**. If you don't have lots of money, you can't afford to gamble, and if you're rich, why would you want to?

—

THE DREADED CAR NOTE: If car payments are gobbling up a substantial portion of your disposable income, you've done a poor job of managing your money. But it's not too late! Thankfully, there is a solution: swallow your pride, sell the nearly new car, and drive a reliable used car that you can more easily afford.

—

THE FOLLY OF CREDIT CARD DEBT: It's been said before in this book and in many other places, but it can't be said too often: If you have high balances on your credit cards that you can't pay off, then you should cut up your credit cards today and start working a second job, if you have to, to pay those balances off completely.

COLLECTIBLES? IT DEPENDS: If you're a collector of things (dolls, baseball cards, stamps, coins, etc.), use common sense. 1. Unless you make your living as a dealer, don't make your collection the centerpiece of your financial plan; 2. Don't expect your collection to dramatically increase in value over time, especially if the product, or variations of the product, are still being manufacture today; 3. Don't expect your collection to be easily turned into cash; 4. Don't necessarily expect your collection to be worth what you paid for it. In other words, collect for fun, not necessarily for profit.

TAKING GOOD CARE OF THE THINGS YOU OWN: Whether it's your car, your lawnmower, your air conditioner, or your kid's tricycle, it will last longer if you keep it cleaned and oiled. A few dollars spent for preventative maintenance today may save thousands of dollars in needless expenses tomorrow.

—

DINING OUT; IS IT WORTH IT? When a kid's meal at the local fast food outlet costs four or five bucks, you simply must ask yourself if it's worth it to eat out.

AND FINALLY

MAKE SURE THAT YOUR FINANCIAL GOALS ARE CONGRUENT WITH YOUR PERSONAL MISSION STATEMENT: and if you don't have a personal mission statement, take a few moments to craft one.

And in Conclusion:
Remember Christ's Promise

"I am come that they might have life,
and that they might have it
more abundantly."
—

John 10:10 KJV